As a Man Thinks

James Allen

Classic Edition (2018)

Updated and Edited
by Richard De A'Morelli

Spectrum Ink Publishing

As a Man Thinks: Classic Edition (2018)

Copyright © 2016, 2018 Spectrum Ink Publishing.
Published simultaneously in Canada and the United States.

First Edition: June 2016
Second Edition: January 2018

All rights reserved. No part of this book may be reproduced or transmitted by any means including photocopying, recording, taping, or digital reproduction, or posted on any blog or website, without the publisher's written consent except for brief quotations embodied in critical articles and reviews.

The views expressed in this work are solely those of the author and do not necessarily reflect the views of the publisher. The publisher hereby disclaims all such views and statements.

ISBN numbers:
978-1-988236-08-7 ~ Mobi/Kindle
978-1-988236-09-4 ~ EPUB Digital
978-1-988236-10-0 ~ Paperback
978-1-988236-44-5 ~ Paperback (Retail)
978-1-988236-12-4 ~ Hardcover

Spectrum Ink Canada
Vancouver, British Columbia

Spectrum Ink USA
San Luis Obispo, California

Spectrum Ink Publishing
http://spectrum.org/books/

Table of Contents

Preface
Why This Book Is Special 5

Chapter 1
The Art and Science of Life 7

Chapter 2
Thought and Character 13

Chapter 3
The Power of Thought on Circumstances 21

Chapter 4
Effect of Thought on Health and Body 37

Chapter 5
Thought and Purpose 43

Chapter 6
The Thought-Factor in Achievement 49

Chapter 7
Visions and Ideals 59

Chapter 8
Serenity 67

Chapter 9
Daily Meditations 73

About the Editor 89
A Message from the Publisher 91
More Books from Spectrum Ink 93

Preface

Why This Book Is Special

This is a special edition of James Allen's most enduring classic, *As a Man Thinketh*. It was developed for a course taught at Virtual University for more than a decade by Richard De A'Morelli, a best-selling author and editor with deep experience in the self-help/inspirational field. Most versions of Allen's book are unedited reprints of his 1903 work, but this Classic Edition includes the full text of his book, carefully edited and restyled for today's readers, as well as insightful tutorials and key points to remember at the end of each chapter. It also includes a bonus chapter at the end of the book presenting a series of daily meditations drawn from Allen's 1913 book, *Meditations for Every Day of the Year*.

This book explores the power of thought and how you can use it to bring prosperity and happiness into your life. You will learn how you are the creator of the conditions that exist in your life, good and bad, and how you can improve those conditions by changing the way you think. Renowned motivational writers, including Dale Carnegie and Norman Vincent Peale, have drawn upon James Allen's practical advice in their own best-selling books, and Inc. Magazine has praised Allen's classic as "one of the top 10 motivational books of all time." Success coach Tony Robbins says it is his favorite book, and he has read it a dozen times.

The wisdom of James Allen reflected in these pages is

as valid today as it was when he published his original work in the early 20th century, providing a foundation for living well and being happy in our hectic modern world. Whether this is your first exposure to his philosophical writings or you are already a fan, this special edition is must reading. Add it to your library, and give it as a gift to friends who may benefit from a wonderfully empowering message that will enable them to change their lives for the better.

Chapter 1

The Art and Science of Life

James Allen was a British philosopher and author of inspirational books in the early twentieth century, best known for *As a Man Thinketh*, published in 1903. He is widely recognized as the grandfather of the self-help and motivational movement. His message of self-empowerment through positive thinking spread around the world and influenced the writings of many prominent authors in the self-help/inspirational field, including Norman Vincent Peale's *The Power of Positive Thinking* and Joshua Liebman's *Peace of Mind*.

Born on November 28, 1864 in Leicester, England, Allen's childhood years were marred by tragedy. Soon after he was born, his father's business failed. In 1880, his father moved to America to start a new life and planned to send for his family after he was established. Two days after he arrived in New York, he was robbed and murdered.

The death of Allen's father drove his family into hard times. At the age of fifteen, Allen was forced to drop out of school, and he spent the next twenty years laboring at clerical jobs. In 1902, he quit his job to pursue writing—an improbable dream for a high school dropout with no education. In leaving behind the security of a paycheck and embarking on a path that seemed doomed to failure, Allen put his faith in the power of the mind and his devout belief that every human being has free will in life, and that we are the masters of our destiny.

To the surprise of many, Allen achieved his goal of becoming a published author. Over the next nine years, he wrote twenty-one inspirational books, all of which are now regarded as classics. He did not seek fame or fortune, and he did not get rich from his writing, but he managed to get by on his meager earnings and never wavered in his belief that the Universe would provide for his needs so that he could continue writing.

After his first book, *From Poverty to Power*, was published, Allen moved to Ilfracombe, a scenic seaside town on the coast of southern England. The rolling hills, cobblestone lanes, and Victorian homes dotting the shoreline provided the tranquil setting he needed for his spiritual contemplation and writing.

Not long after moving to Ilfracombe, Allen began writing his second book, *As a Man Thinketh*. It reflected the essence of his belief in the power of mind and man's ability to determine his own fate. But Allen was not happy with the first drafts. It took months of encouragement from his wife, Lily, before he finally sent the manuscript off to a publisher. It would become his greatest and most enduring success, offering his reflections on life and man's quest to understand his purpose and relationship to the Universe.

James Allen lived the modest, ascetic life of a mystic as described in the writings of the Russian novelist and philosopher Leo Tolstoy, whom Allen idolized. He followed a path of moderation, self-discipline, respect for all living things, and voluntary poverty. Like Tolstoy, Allen focused on life's most profound goals: to be happy and positive, to live in the present, and to find the silver lining in every cloud. He was an avid learner, cherished knowledge, welcomed new ideas, and embraced manual labor. He was grateful for the good things life bestowed on him, no matter how small, and he followed his own teachings, expressing positive thoughts and actions in his life at all times.

A typical day began at dawn with a walk through the rocky hills overlooking the sea. He would meditate for an hour and spend the rest of the morning writing. His afternoons were spent gardening, and in the evenings, he had deep conversations with friends, admirers, and students who traveled from all over Europe to discuss his writings.

One of Allen's friends described him as "a frail-looking little man, with a mass of flowing black hair. I recall him in the black, velvet suit he always wore in the evenings. He would talk quietly to a small group of us—English, French, Austrian, and Indian—of meditation, of philosophy, of Tolstoy or Buddha, and of killing nothing, not even a mouse in the garden."

Allen's career as a philosopher and author ended abruptly. Just nine years after his first book was published, he died in his sleep at the age of 48.

After his death, his wife Lily recalled that "He wrote when he had a message, and it became a message only when he had lived it out in his own life and knew it was good."

James Allen was the proverbial "messenger with the right message for the right time." His writings emerged as the strict doctrines of Protestantism in Europe had begun to soften. Offering an uplifting philosophy of hope that blended Christianity with the mystical teachings of the East, he looked beyond the harsh doctrine that man is born, lives and dies in sin, and is doomed to suffer in the purgatory of Earth. Instead, he offered a benevolent alternative—an optimistic view that man is inherently good, and the seeds of divine wisdom dwell within us all.

The erosion of Protestant dogma brought new interest in philosophy and religion, which blossomed in the early 1900s. As the tide moved toward a more liberal view of the human dilemma, science and religion began to reconcile, and *The Origin of Species* by Charles Darwin was published. Darwin, too, recognized that the power of thought can shape our lives for better or worse, as evidenced by his observation: "The highest possible stage in moral culture is when we recognize that we ought to control our thoughts."

Allen's writings on the power of the mind and free will have helped millions of readers to understand that some people express good and positive qualities; others choose to be negative or evil. We decide upon our course from day to day, and we can change that course at any time. All our successes and failures, our joys and sorrows, our achievements and disappointments in life, are of our own making, the product of our individual thoughts and actions.

James Allen blended traditional Western philosophy and Eastern mysticism into an inspiring message of hope. The ideas expressed in his writings are not original, which is not a surprise, as Ecclesiastes 1:9 reminds us: "There is nothing new under the sun." Allen draws from a variety of sources, especially Buddhism. For instance, *The Dhammapada*, a Buddhist scripture from the third century B.C., tells us, "All we are is the result of what we have thought," and Allen writes, "As a man thinketh in his heart, so is he."

Today, Allen's enduring advice reminds us that even in a world torn by injustice, bigotry, poverty, and strife, we can make a conscious choice to live peaceful, harmonious lives, and to do so, we need only commit to expressing positive thoughts and actions in our daily affairs.

"Yes, humanity surges with uncontrolled passion, is tumultuous with ungoverned grief, is blown about by anxiety and doubt," writes Allen. "Only the wise man whose thoughts are pure and controlled makes the winds and the storms of the soul obey him."

I was introduced to *As a Man Thinketh* on my tenth birthday, when I received a copy from my sixth-grade English teacher. I didn't understand Allen's words then, but his book would have a major influence on my life as time went by. It inspired me to begin writing at age 14; to pursue the dream of being a freelance writer; and to believe that I could succeed. I went on to publish a dozen books, and all my early works were in the self-help/inspirational genre.

Years later, I developed a self-help course based on *As a Man* Thinketh, which I taught at Virtual University. The first few times I offered the class, some students indicated that the book was difficult to follow. The writing style in the early 1900s was more verbose and complex than what present-day readers expect, and some women in the class disliked the book's male-centric focus. With careful editing, I restyled the book and endeavored to make it gender-neutral. I also added helpful study notes at the end of each chapter. My students reacted positively and suggested that I should publish this updated version. At last, I have found the time to do that.

    I hope you will enjoy this Classic Edition and that it will open your eyes and heart to the remarkable power and potential of the human mind.

Chapter 2

Thought and Character

The principle, "As a man thinks in his heart, so he is" (Proverbs 23:7), not only encompasses the whole of a man's being but pertains to every condition and circumstance in his life. A man is literally what he thinks. His character is the complete sum of all his thoughts. Every joyous and desirable condition in his life, every action and deed, every habit, and every dire predicament is a reflection of his thoughts and of his own making.

As a plant springs from a seed and could not otherwise exist, every act of a man springs from the seeds of thought and could not have appeared without them. This applies equally to acts that are "spontaneous" and "unplanned" as well as acts deliberately executed.

Action is the blossom of thought, and its fruits are joy and suffering. Thus, a man reaps what he sows. He harvests the sweet and bitter fruit of the seeds he has planted in the fertile garden of his mind and soul.

> *Thought in the mind has made us what we are.*
> *By thought, a man builds and shapes his life.*
> *If a man's mind has dark and impure thoughts,*
> *Pain comes on him as comes the wheel behind the ox.*
> *If a man endures in purity of thought,*
> *Joy follows him as surely as his own shadow.*

Man's life and affairs are governed by natural laws. Nothing happens in life by random chance or coincidence. The Law of Cause and Effect is absolute and certain in the hidden realm of thought, just as it is in the visible world of material things. A spiritually enlightened character cannot be acquired from a book or course. It does not develop overnight or happen by chance. It is the end result of diligent effort and faithful devotion to right thinking that evolves from dwelling on pure and wholesome thoughts. A dishonorable or cruel, violent character, by the same process, is the inevitable result of continually harboring dark, indulgent, and destructive thoughts.

Man is made or unmade by himself. In the armory of thought, he forges the weapons by which he destroys himself; but he also fashions the tools by which he builds heavenly mansions of joy, strength, and peace for himself. By making the right choices and putting right thoughts into action, he can aspire to the lofty goal of spiritual enlightenment and divine perfection. By the abuse of thought, and by putting thought to work in destructive ways, he descends to the lowest and darkest levels of human nature. Between these two extremes are all the grades of character, and man is their maker and master.

Of all the beautiful truths pertaining to the soul that have been re-discovered and brought to light, none is more uplifting or inspiring of courage, hope, and confidence than this: You are the master of thought, the molder of character, and the maker and shaper of your condition, environment, and destiny.

As a being of power, intelligence, and love, and the maker of your own thoughts, you hold the key to every situation in life. Within you dwells a transformative and life-changing power by which you can make yourself what you will.

A man is always the master of his life and circumstances, even in his weakest moments, and his most desperate and depraved states. In his weakness and degradation, he is the foolish master who misgoverns his household, squanders his fortune, alienates his loved ones, and lives out his life in the darkest corners of his soul. When he begins to reflect upon his condition and search for an understanding of the laws upon which his character and environment are based, he becomes the wise master, directing his energies with intelligence and focusing his thoughts on worthwhile issues. In this way, he becomes the conscious master. But it can only happen when he discovers that the laws of thought are at work in his life, and he learns their proper application. That discovery is only possible through self-analysis and experience.

Only by much searching and mining can gold and diamonds be obtained, and only by digging deep into the mine of your soul can you find every truth that shaped your character and the circumstances in your life. By searching in your soul for these truths, you will discover you are the maker of your character, the molder of your life, and the builder of your destiny.

You can find unerring proof of these truths if you watch and alter your thoughts. Observe the effects of your thoughts upon you and others. Notice their effects on your life and circumstances. You will see the link between cause and effect—and thus the reason all things that happen in your life—by patient observation and investigation. Use every experience, even the most trivial, everyday occurrences, as a way to gain that knowledge of yourself. From that knowledge will come the fruits of Understanding, Wisdom, and Power.

By engaging in these actions and living your life according to the laws of thought, you will find that the law is absolute: *He who asks receives; the one who seeks finds; and to the one who knocks, the door will be opened* (Luke 11:10). Only by patience, practice, and ceaseless application of this law can you enter and explore the Temple of Knowledge.

Insights and Points to Remember

In this chapter on *Thought and Character*, we are introduced to the central premise intertwined in every chapter of this book:

> **You are what you think, and you can change your life, for better or worse, by changing your thoughts.**

The degree of change you can expect will correspond to the effort you put into guiding your thoughts from negative to positive, and how determined you are to remain positive. Small changes in your thought processes can yield small improvements in your circumstances. Major changes can bring immediate, dramatic, and gratifying improvements on every level —physical, emotional, mental, and spiritual.

Of course, not everyone follows the happy path to positive thinking described in this book. Some people go the opposite way and fall into the grips of negative thinking brought on by myriad fears and doubts that inundate us every day and that we express in a multitude of ways as anger, insecurity, jealousy, depression, self-loathing, obsession, and addictive habits. Becoming mired in this thinking can throw one's life into a downward spiral of turmoil or keep a person trapped in this tragic place indefinitely.

We often hear people say, "Think positive!" You may respond, "Yeah, whatever!" and give it no credence. After all, it's just a saying; a pleasant-sounding cliche. Or you might say, "I think positive about winning a million dollars in the lotto, but it never happens!" Merely hoping something wonderful will happen is not positive thinking.

In the pages to come, you will learn it takes an understanding of the laws of the mind and diligent perseverance to keep the mind focused on the positive from hour to hour, day to day, and week to week. It is easy to let doubts and fears about trivial events in our lives color our thoughts, especially when we have spent years trapped in hopelessness and expecting failure at whatever we attempt to do.

In my self-help book, *Live Well, Be Happy* (Spectrum

Ink Publishing, 2016), I explain: "A few drops of positive energy won't have much effect if you are living in a muddy swamp of negativity. This is why, when a person says, 'But I meditated and I tried to hold positive thoughts for five minutes!' nothing comes of it, and they conclude positive thinking doesn't work. Before positive thinking can produce results, you need to pull one foot out of the swamp and plant it on solid ground...you then can begin the task of banishing negativity from your environment and cultivating fruitful seeds in your garden."

But first things first—let's establish what the power of positive thought is all about and consider some credible evidence that it not only works but can work miracles in your life! We have ample evidence from psychologists and the traditional medical community to support the reality that our thoughts do affect us on every level: physical, emotional, mental, and spiritual. Even the Mayo Clinic, a renowned medical facility and hardly a bastion of metaphysical thinking, extols the benefits of positive thinking. An article bylined by the Mayo Clinic Staff reports:

"Is your glass half-empty or half-full? How you answer this age-old question about positive thinking may reflect your outlook on life, your attitude toward yourself, and whether you are optimistic or pessimistic—and it may even affect your health . . . Indeed, some studies show that personality traits like optimism and pessimism can affect many areas of your health and well-being."

The article confirms that scientists are now investigating the effects of positive thought and optimism on health, and the benefits thus far proven include:

— *increased life span*
— *lower rates of depression*
— *lower levels of distress*
— *greater resistance to common colds*
— *improved psychological well-being*
— *better physical health*
— *reduced risk of death from heart disease*
— *better coping skills during stressful times*

The article concludes that it is not clear why individuals who practice positive thinking experience these health benefits. But James Allen knew the reason more than a century ago when he wrote *As a Man Thinketh*. He was not the first to teach readers about the power of thought on one's mind and circumstances, but his little book became an enduring classic that has inspired millions of readers around the world over the years.

Moving forward, we must remember positive thinking, like its negative counterpart, is pure habit. It takes time to learn, but far less time to unlearn and slip back into old habits. So even if you make a solid effort, and you succeed at bringing positive thought into your life, you must guard against falling back. The climb to the top of the mountain is arduous and requires great effort. If a climber slips, the fall is sudden and requires no effort. It simply happens, it happens quickly, and the consequences are dramatic and unfortunate.

In the next chapter, we will explore how positive thinking can influence your life, your environment, your future prospects for happiness and success, and your spiritual destiny.

Chapter 3

The Power of Thought on Circumstances

A man's mind is like a garden, and his thoughts are seeds waiting to take root. His mind can be intelligently cultivated or allowed to run wild. Either way, his thoughts must, and will, bring forth. If no useful seeds are planted, an abundance of useless weeds will grow and continue to produce more of the same.

Just as a gardener cultivates his plot, keeping it free of weeds and growing the flowers and fruits he desires, so a man must tend the garden of his mind, weeding out useless and impure thoughts, and cultivating to perfection his choice of pure and useful thoughts. By tending to the thought-seeds he plants, he discovers that he is the master gardener of his soul and the director of his life and destiny. He also discovers the laws of thought at work in himself, and he grows to understand with increasing clarity how his mind and thought forces work to shape his character, circumstances, and destiny.

> *Mind is the Master power that molds and makes.*
> *Man is Mind, and evermore he takes*
> *The tool of Thought, and, shaping what he wills*
> *Brings forth a thousand joys, a thousand ills.*
> *He thinks in secret, and it comes to pass:*
> *His environment is but his looking glass.*

Thought and character are one. A man's thoughts shape his character, and his character will cause him to seek out circumstances that produce more of the same thoughts, reinforcing his character. Just as character manifests itself and can only be discovered through environment and circumstance, the outer conditions of a man's life will always be in sync with his inner state. His character mirrors his inner state, and his thoughts further strengthen that image. This does not mean his circumstances at a given time reflect his entire character, but rather, they are so intimately connected with some vital thought process within himself that, for the time being, they are indispensable to his development.

Every man is where he is by the law of his being. The thoughts that form his character have brought him to this time and place. In the arrangement of his life, there is no element of chance. According to the law of cause and effect, every effect has a cause, and there is no such thing as coincidence. All that happens is a predictable working of an unerring natural law. This is just as true of the man who feels "out of harmony" with his surroundings as of the man who is content and thrives in his environment.

Man is a progressive and evolving being. He is at his current position in life so that he can learn and grow. As he learns the spiritual lesson that each life circumstance holds for him, that condition passes away and other circumstances rise to take its place.

As long as you believe yourself to be a creature of

outside conditions, your life will be buffeted by circumstances. When you realize that you can control the hidden soil and seeds of your being, and that you are the maker of the thoughts out of which your circumstances grow, you will become the rightful master of yourself and your destiny.

Circumstances spring from thought—that simple truth is well known to everyone who has practiced any form of meditation and self-control. We will notice that the alteration in our circumstances is in exact ratio to our altered mental condition. We can see the proof of this in our everyday living: When you diligently apply yourself to remedy the defects in your character, you will make swift and marked progress, and you will pass rapidly through the steps of inner growth.

The soul attracts what it harbors, what it loves, what it desires, and what it fears. It can ascend to the height of its cherished aspirations or descend to the lowest depths of its darkest desires. Circumstances are the means by which the soul receives its own.

Every thought-seed sown or allowed to fall into the mind, and that you allow to take root, produces its own and sooner or later blossoms into action. Each seed that sprouts bears its own fruit of opportunity and circumstance. Good thoughts bear good fruit, and bad thoughts bear bad fruit.

The outer world of circumstance shapes itself to the inner world of thought. Pleasant and unpleasant external conditions are factors that make for the ultimate good of the individual and that man's destiny. As the reaper of our own harvest, we learn both by bliss and suffering in our lives.

A man does not fall into depravity or find his way into jail by the tyranny of fate or circumstance. Rather, it happens because he follows the path of negative thoughts and base desires. A pure-minded man does not suddenly fall into crime propelled by an arbitrary external force. His susceptibility to criminal thought was a seed planted in the mind long ago and secretly fostered in the heart. When the hour of opportunity arrived, that seed flowered and its gathered power was revealed.

**Circumstance does not make
or break you. It reveals you to yourself.**

A man cannot descend into vice or depravity unless those thoughts are in his mind. No such conditions can exist in his life unless his thoughts give them substance; and suffering can only occur when those thoughts and the resulting circumstances cause his mind to descend into vice and negative inclinations. Likewise, a man cannot ascend into virtue and its pure happiness without continually planting the seeds of virtuous aspirations. You, therefore, as master of your thoughts, are the maker of yourself, the shaper of your environment, and the author of your destiny.

Even at birth, the soul comes to its own. Through every step of its earthly pilgrimage, it attracts those conditions that reveal itself, reflecting its own purity and impurity, its strength and weakness.

A man does not attract what he wants but what he is.

His whims, fancies, and ambitions are thwarted at every step; but his innermost thoughts and desires are fed with their own food, be it clean or foul. The "divinity that shapes our ends" is in ourselves—it is our very self. We are shackled only by ourselves.

Thought and action are the jailers of Destiny, limiting and imprisoning us. Yet, thought and action are also the angels of freedom, liberating and inspiring us to move forward in life to fulfill our spiritual destiny. A man does not get what he wishes and prays for, but rather, what he earns or deserves. Our wishes and prayers are only answered when they harmonize with our thoughts and actions.

In the light of this, what is the meaning of "fighting against circumstances"? It means that we are continually revolting against an effect that is outside and all around us, but at the same time, we are nourishing and preserving its cause in our heart. That cause may take the form of a conscious vice or an unconscious weakness; but whatever it is, it stubbornly retards the efforts of its possessor and thus requires a remedy.

As human beings, we are eager to improve our circumstances. Yet, we are unwilling to improve ourselves. Thus, we remain bound. One who does not shrink from hard work and who remains dedicated to a goal, willing to self-sacrifice to achieve that goal, will always accomplish the object on which his heart is set. This is true of earthly as well as heavenly things. Even the man whose sole object in life is to gain wealth must be ready and willing to exert much effort and make personal sacrifices before he can accomplish his quest. The man who would realize a strong and spiritually enlightened life must be ready and willing to do the same.

Here is a man who is wretchedly poor. He is anxious to improve his surroundings and his home comforts. Yet, he complains about his circumstances, he shirks his work and believes that he is justified in deceiving his employer on the notion that he is underpaid. Such a man does not understand the simplest principles that are the basis of true prosperity. He is not only unfit to rise out of his unhappy situation, but he is attracting to himself greater misery and suffering by dwelling in and acting out dishonest, deceptive, and negative thoughts.

Here is a rich man who is the victim of a painful and chronic disease caused by gluttony. He is willing to donate vast sums of money to cure the disease, but he will not give up his gluttonous desires. He wants to gratify his taste for unhealthy foods and have his good health as well. Such a man is unfit to have health because he has not yet learned the first principles of a healthy life.

Here is an employer who resorts to crooked methods to avoid paying taxes, and he reduces his workers' wages hoping to make higher profits. Such a man is unfit for prosperity because he has not yet learned the first principles of generosity. When he finds himself bankrupt, both in reputation and riches, he blames other people or "bad luck," not realizing he is the architect of his condition. He brought failure upon himself by his thoughts and his actions which reflected those thoughts.

These examples merely illustrate that a man is the cause of his circumstances, although it is often unconscious. While striving for positive goals, he continually frustrates their accomplishment by harboring thoughts and desires that cannot possibly harmonize with that end. He cannot expect to succeed when his thoughts are on failure and he acts in ways that justify his thinking and guarantees he will fail.

We can look around and see many other examples where a man is the cause of his own conditions and misery. But you, the reader, can trace the action of the laws of thought in your own mind and life. Until this is done, mere examples and reading facts in a book will not inspire you to change or bring you closer to the fulfillment of the goals you seek or your destiny.

In your life, your circumstances may be so complicated, your thoughts may be so deeply rooted, or the conditions of happiness you seek may differ so greatly from your circumstances, your thoughts, or the desires of another person who has sway in your life, your soul condition cannot be judged by an outsider who views your external circumstances.

A man might be honest in certain ways yet suffer setbacks and loss. Another man might be dishonest in certain ways yet acquire wealth. People who do not understand the laws of thought form hasty conclusions—they assume that one man fails because of his honesty, and the other prospers because of his dishonesty. These superficial judgments assume that the dishonest person is almost totally corrupt, and the honest person is almost entirely virtuous. This is rarely the case. The dishonest man may have virtues that the other does not possess; and the honest man may have obnoxious traits or vices absent in the other. The honest man reaps the good results of his honest thoughts and acts, yet, he also brings upon himself the sufferings that spring from his vices. The dishonest man likewise brings his own suffering and happiness.

It is human vanity to amuse ourselves with the notion that a man suffers because of his virtue. Those who do not understand the laws of thought imagine that virtue is weakness, and the virtuous man who suffers defeat lacks fortitude and blind ambition. But we cannot declare that our sufferings are the result of our good qualities and not of our bad until we have rooted out every negative thought from our mind and washed every dark blemish from our soul. On the way to that state of spiritual purification, we will have discovered that the spiritual order of the universe is just and unerring: we cannot reap good for evil or evil for good. When we recognize this, we will look back upon our past ignorance and know that our life is, and always was, justly ordered. We will realize that all past experiences, good and bad, were the equitable workings of our evolving yet unevolved self.

Good thoughts and actions can never produce bad results. Bad thoughts and actions can never produce good results. Nothing but corn can come from planting corn, and nothing from nettles but nettles. Some men understand this law in the natural world and work with it. But few understand its application to morals, although its operation in that realm is just as simple and undeviating, and so they do not cooperate with it.

Suffering is always the effect of wrong thought in some direction. It is a sign that a man is out of harmony with himself and the law of his being. The purpose of suffering is to purify and burn out all that is useless and impure, and to move us along the path from imperfection to sublime perfection. The person who is pure no longer suffers.

The circumstances in a man's life that cause him to suffer are the result of his thoughts being in disarray and impure. The circumstances that bestow blessedness and serenity are the result of his thoughts being harmonious and pure. Such blessings come from right thoughts and right acts. Wretchedness, not a lack of wealth or material possessions, is the measure of wrong thought. A man can be rich yet cursed; or he may be blessed and poor. Blessedness and riches are only joined together when the riches are rightly and wisely used. A poor man only descends into wretchedness when he believes his condition is unjustly imposed.

Indigence, or extreme poverty, and its counterpart, indulgence, which happens when a man has too much of something, are two extremes of wretchedness. They are both unnatural and the fruit of unhealthy thinking. A person is not rightly conditioned until he is happy, healthy, and prosperous. Happiness, health, and prosperity are the natural result of a balance of the inner with the outer and of a man with his surroundings.

A man only begins to live when he ceases to whine, grovel, and hate, and he commences to search for the hidden justice that regulates all life. As he adapts his mind to that regulating factor, he stops blaming others as the cause of his condition, and he fortifies himself with strong and noble thoughts. He ceases to fight and kick against circumstances but instead begins to use them as aids to motivate greater progress and discover the hidden powers and possibilities within himself.

Law, not confusion, is the dominating principle in the Universe. Justice, not injustice, is the soul and substance of life. Integrity, not corruption, is the empowering force in the spiritual government of the world. This being true, you will find that the Universe is right by righting yourself. During the process of putting yourself right, you will discover that as you change your thoughts towards things and other people, things and other people will change towards you.

You can confirm that your thoughts and desires control your circumstances, and your circumstances reinforce your thoughts and desires, by diligent self-analysis and introspection. If you radically alter your thoughts, you will be amazed at the rapid improvement it will bring about in the material conditions of your life.

People amuse themselves believing that dark and impure thoughts they would never openly admit to thinking can be kept secret. They cannot. Such thoughts rapidly manifest as desires, and those desires soon crystallize into habits. Those habits solidify into sensation seeking and addiction, which develop into circumstances of depravity and destitution. Impure thoughts of every kind crystallize into confusing and disabling habits, which solidify into circumstances of discord and disease. Thoughts of fear, doubt, and indecision crystallize into weak, cowardly, and irresolute habits, which solidify into circumstances of failure, dependence, and poverty.

Lazy and unfocused thoughts crystallize into habits of apathy and pessimism, which solidify into circumstances of helplessness and defeat. Hateful and condemning thoughts crystallize into habits of accusation and violence, which solidify into circumstances of cruelty and persecution. Selfish thoughts of all kinds crystallize into habits of self-seeking and greed, which solidify into circumstances of deprivation and loss, and we discover that what we most desire in life is taken away.

On the other hand, beautiful thoughts crystallize into habits of optimism, honesty and compassion, which solidify into bright, sunny circumstances. Pure thoughts crystallize into habits of moderation and self-control, which solidify into circumstances of balance and peace. Thoughts of confidence and self-reliance crystallize into noble habits, which solidify into circumstances of freedom and success.

Energetic thoughts crystallize into habits of hard work and accomplishment, which solidify into circumstances of prosperity and attainment. Gentle, forgiving thoughts crystallize into habits of kindness and compassion, which solidify into secure and harmonious circumstances. Loving and unselfish thoughts crystallize into habits of affection and generosity, which solidify into circumstances of divine love and spiritual enlightenment.

Any train of thought you persist in—good or bad—will have a distinct and noticeable effect on your character, which in turn, will have an effect on your circumstances. While you cannot directly choose your circumstances in life, you can choose your thoughts, and so indirectly but surely, you can shape your circumstances.

The law of cause and effect means that every man will gratify the thoughts upon which he dwells. Life will present opportunities that will speedily bring to the surface both his good and evil thoughts and then reward them.

Let a man cease from destructive and immoral thoughts, and all the world will soften towards him and be ready to help him. Let him give up weak and pessimistic thoughts, and he will see opportunities spring up all around to reward his strong resolve. Let him think good and pure thoughts, and he will never be shackled by despair and shame—his destiny will be aglow with happiness, success, and tranquility as the just rewards for his endeavors.

The world is your kaleidoscope, and the varying combinations of colors displayed from moment to moment will be the exquisitely adjusted pictures of your ever-moving thoughts. As your thoughts change, what you attract will change. What you see around you will change, and the conditions of your life will change, for good or bad, to reflect your altered outlook.

> *You will be what you will to be.*
> *Let failure find its false content.*
> *In the circumstances of your environment*
> *Your spirit yearns to be free.*
> *It masters time, it conquers space;*
> *It cows that boastful trickster Chance,*
> *And dispels the tyrant Circumstance,*
> *Uncrowning it to fill a servant's place.*
> *The human Will, that force unseen,*
> *The offspring of a deathless Soul,*
> *Can hew a way to any goal.*
> *Be not impatient in delay,*
> *But wait as one who understands;*
> *When spirit rises and commands,*
> *The universe is ready to obey.*

Insights and Points to Remember

This chapter introduces the concept that the human mind is a garden, and our thoughts are seeds we plant in it as we go through life. Positive thoughts are likened to sweet corn, and negative thoughts are akin to bitter herbs. Our thoughts day to day determine which seeds we plant, and those seeds will blossom into circumstances that shape our lives, for better or worse.

The point of this lesson is clear, but it is a principle many people forget as they struggle through the stresses and strains of daily life. We cannot expect to harvest sweet corn if we plant bitter herbs. For thoughts to translate into positive actions and outcomes, we must plant the useful thought-seeds and not let weeds take root. The weeds are negative thoughts that set unwholesome and self-destructive energies in motion around us.

The teaching "Man reaps what he sows" can be traced to a Biblical verse, and it has been integrated into many philosophies and thought systems since then. It is another way of saying that the natural law of cause and effect governs everything within the physical universe as well as the spiritual realm. For every action, there is a reaction; for every thought, a corresponding action, and every seed planted in our spiritual garden bears the fruit of what we have planted.

This chapter reveals another important teaching: Thought and character are one. We are told: "A man's thoughts shape his character, and his character will cause him to seek out circumstances that produce more of the same thoughts, reinforcing his character."

In other words, we become what we think, and what we become causes us to think more of the same thoughts. Thus, negative thinking can become a vicious cycle that drags us deeper and deeper into anger, despair, and other undesirable conditions. But when we express positive thoughts, it shapes our character, accentuates virtuous qualities, encourages further positive thinking, and attracts desirable and pleasant effects and circumstances into our lives.

The terms *positive* and *negative, and good* and *bad,* are used in a broad, philosophical sense in this book. We avoid subjective, moral judgments and accept that what is good for one person may be undesirable for another. Likewise, what might be good for you at this moment in time may not be right for you at another time, depending on your life circumstances and your emotional, intellectual, and spiritual state of being.

After you have read through this chapter, think back over the major highs and lows of your life in recent years. See if you can identify the cause-and-effect relationship between your thoughts and actions, and the results you obtained. Consider how your thoughts and actions influenced the outcomes and apply those insights to your circumstances in the here and now. Are you setting yourself up for disappointment and failure right now, or are you on a positive path, taking constructive actions that will pave the road for future success and happiness?

Chapter 4

Effect of Thought on Health and Body

The body is the servant of the mind. It obeys the mind's directives, whether they are chosen consciously or unconsciously expressed. When the mind expresses negative or destructive thoughts, the body becomes vulnerable to disease and decay. The longer those unsavory thoughts are expressed, the stronger their effect and the deeper the body sinks into ill health. When the mind expresses positive and beautiful thoughts, the body radiates vitality and beauty.

Health and disease, like circumstances, are rooted in thought. Unhealthy thoughts, such as anger, fear, hatred, obsession, and other negative emotions, will express themselves through an unhealthy body. Thoughts of fear have been known to kill a person as quickly as a fatal bullet, and such thoughts are slowly but surely killing millions of people today. People who live in fear of disease are the ones who get it. Anxiety demoralizes the whole body, making it susceptible to disease. Impure thoughts, even if not indulged, will overload and shatter the nervous system.

Strong, pure, and happy thoughts strengthen the body and promote vitality, wellness, and a healthy constitution. The body is a delicate and fluid instrument; it responds readily to the thoughts to which it is exposed. Habits of thought will produce their own effects on it, for good or bad.

As long as a man propagates negative and unevolved thoughts, he will continue to have disease and physical ailments. As long as he clings to base and unhealthy desires, he will suffer addictions and their detrimental effects on body, mind, and soul. Out of a defiled mind evolves a defiled life and a corrupt body. From a clean heart comes a wholesome life and a clean body. Thought is the wellspring of all action, and the results of those actions create our circumstances. Make the fountain pure and all that a man is and aspires to be will be pure.

A change of diet will not help a man who will not change his thoughts, because his thoughts will precipitate actions, and those actions will cause him to overeat and gain weight, regardless of what he decides to eat. When a man makes his thoughts pure, his body and mind are in harmony and he no longer craves food or overeats.

Clean thoughts make clean habits. Clean habits make a healthy body and a vibrant spirit. The man who has strengthened and purified his thoughts is above fearing the possible effects of a malevolent microbe.

As a man protects his body, so it is essential that he guard his mind. As he would protect his hands while using a saw, he must protect his mind from idle and negative thoughts. Renew the body, beautify the mind. Exercise the body in healthy ways, and in the same way, engage the mind in healthy discourse. Make the mind pure and you dispel emotional dis-ease; make the emotions pure, and you rid dis-ease from the body.

Thoughts of malice, jealousy, depression, and failure suck the life force from the body, leaving it depleted and making the owner of that body sickly, prone to aches and pains, and exhausted. A dour face does not come onto a person by chance—it is made by dour thoughts. Wrinkles on the face are created by folly, passion, and fear in a man's day-to-day thoughts.

I know a woman ninety-six years old who has the bright, innocent face of a girl. I know a man who is thirty, and his face is drawn in stark contours, making him look very old and tired. The one is the result of a sweet and sunny disposition; the other is the outcome of passion and discontent.

You cannot have a sweet and wholesome home unless you open the windows to admit the air and let sunshine into your rooms. A healthy body and a bright, happy countenance can only result by opening the mind and admitting thoughts of joy and good will, and by striving for tranquility.

As a man grows older, on his face, we see wrinkles made by sympathy. On another man, we see thin, light creases made by strong and pure thought. On yet another, we see deep lines carved by passion. We can easily distinguish one man from another. Those who have lived frantic lives full of stress and angry passions have deep lines carved by the intensity of their emotions and unsatisfied desires. For those who have lived righteous and peaceful lives, age is calm and softly mellowed, like the setting sun. I saw a philosopher on his death bed. He was not old, except in chronological years. He died as sweetly and peacefully as he had lived.

There is no better physician than bright and cheerful thought for dissipating the ills and impurities of the body, and there is no comforter greater than good will for dispersing anger, grief, and sorrow. To live continually in thoughts of ill-will, greed, envy, and fear of failing is to be confined in a self-made prison. But to think well of all, to be cheerful with all, to patiently learn to search for the good in all, in such pure and unselfish thoughts are the very portals of heaven. To dwell day to day in thoughts of love and peace toward every person and creature we encounter will bring abounding joy and peace to the man who thinks them.

Insights and Points to Remember

This chapter examines the power of mind over body. It discusses how your thoughts can affect your health, and how your physical health reflects your mental and emotional state. The main take away is that "the body obeys the mind's directives. When the mind expresses negative or destructive thoughts, the body becomes vulnerable to disease and decay. When the mind expresses positive and beautiful thoughts, the body radiates vitality and beauty."

Earlier, we touched on how thoughts and moods affect the body in powerful ways. These effects have been acknowledged by medical experts and documented by a plethora of scientific research in recent years. Some of the many healthful benefits of positive thinking include lower levels of stress, a longer life span, increased resistance to the common cold, and reduced risk of death from cardiovascular disease.

A study published in *JAMA Psychiatry* reports on a team of Danish researchers who found that people with pessimistic views are 55% more likely to die in the next decade. Men with pessimistic outlooks were much more likely to die prematurely. The study involved 604 hospital patients in Denmark, and it also discovered that those with positive outlooks were 58% more likely to live at least another five years.

Dr. Suzanne Segerstrom, a University of Kentucky psychology professor, conducted a study of 124 freshman law students to determine if there is a connection between optimism and the immune system. She published her findings in *Brain, Behavior, and Immunity*. The research confirmed that students who exhibited positive thinking had greater cell-mediated immunity. Segerstrom also found that pessimistic thinking had an adverse effect on immune cell response. Thus, negative thinking can make you susceptible to illness and disease. This lends credence to the irony that people who fear getting cancer are most often the ones who get it.

A study reported in *Circulation*, a journal of the American Heart Association, found that positive thinking is a deterrent to heart disease. Researchers confirmed that optimistic people were less likely to develop coronary heart disease. Another study found that people who had higher levels of optimism had a 73% lower risk of heart failure compared with those who were pessimistic.

Research on adults over the age of 60 reported in the *Canadian Medical Association Journal* confirmed that seniors who indulge in pessimism and negative thinking experience more health problems and decreased mobility performing day-to-day tasks. They were 78% more likely than their optimistic counterparts to develop mobility and functioning problems.

Recent science has dispelled any doubt that the mind can have a powerful effect, good or bad, on an individual's health and well-being. Negative thinking could be making you sick or killing you! If you didn't already have good reasons to elevate your thoughts to a more level in daily life, you can add the precious gifts of good health, vitality, slower aging, and a longer life to the list of incentives!

Chapter 5

Thought and Purpose

Thought is meaningless without purpose. Until thought is linked with a purpose, it is wasted energy, and there can be no intelligent accomplishment. With the majority of men, the seeds of thought are thrown about at random and allowed to drift on the ocean of life. Usually, only random results occur, and most of the seeds go to waste. Aimlessness is a vice, and a man who desires to steer clear of catastrophe and destruction must not let himself drift idly, wasting time and energy. Time is precious. We will never get a chance to relive the present hour or the present day again. Therefore, make the most of it, and let each day bring you closer to peace, happiness, and the realization of your spiritual destiny.

Those who have no central purpose in their life easily fall prey to worries, fears, and self-pity. All of these negative thoughts are indications of weakness and will lead, just as surely as though deliberately planned, to failure, unhappiness, and loss. Weakness cannot persist in a power-evolving universe.

Conceive of a legitimate purpose in your heart. Fix a goal in your mind, and once the goal is clear, set out to accomplish it. Make this purpose the central focal point of your thoughts. It may take the form of a spiritual ideal or a worldly objective or goal, depending on your nature at the present moment. Whichever it is, steadily focus the power of your thought upon what you have set out to attain. Make this purpose your supreme duty and devote yourself to its attainment each day. Do not allow your thoughts to wander to distractions, imaginings, or wishful thinking. This is the enlightened road to self-control and true concentration of thought.

Even if you fail again and again to accomplish your purpose, which will happen until you have replaced weakness with strength, the strength of character gained will be the measure of your true success, and this will form a new starting point for your future power and victories.

Those who are not prepared to undertake a great purpose should fix their thoughts on the faultless performance of their day-to-day activities, no matter how insignificant those tasks may be. Only in this way can a man gather and focus his thoughts. Such focusing is necessary to develop resolution, motivation, and energy. Once this is done, every goal that a man can imagine is within the realm of possibility and can be accomplished.

The weakest soul, recognizing its own weakness and believing strength can only be developed by effort and practice, will begin to exert itself immediately. Adding effort to effort, patience to patience, and strength to strength, the soul will continually develop and in time, it will grow infinitely strong.

As the physically weak man can make himself strong by

careful and patient training and a faithful exercise regimen, so the man whose thoughts are weak can make them strong by will power and by faithfully practicing right thinking.

Letting go of laziness and strengthening the mind to overcome weakness and habits is the first step that a man must take to begin thinking with purpose. To think with the mind focused and fully energized is to enter the ranks of those strong and determined individuals who recognize that failure is merely a delay on the pathway to attainment, and one that can and must be overcome. The strong man makes all conditions serve him. He thinks strongly, attempts fearlessly, and accomplishes masterfully.

Having decided upon your lofty purpose or goal, chart a straight pathway to its achievement. Begin today, without procrastination, and do not succumb to distractions. Put aside all doubts and fears—they are disintegrating thought forces that break up the straight line of effort, rendering it crooked, ineffectual, and useless. Thoughts of doubt and fear accomplish nothing and always lead to failure. Purpose, energy, the will to achieve—all these strong and motivating thoughts wither and cease when doubt and fear creep in.

The will to accomplish springs from the knowledge that we can do it. Doubt and fear are the great enemies of knowledge and accomplishment. The man who encourages these negative thought-seeds or sees them in his own thoughts and does not weed them out defeats himself at every step.

Conquer your doubt and fear, and you will conquer

failure. Your every thought will be allied with power. All difficulties will be bravely met, all obstacles will be overcome. Your purposes are the seeds in your garden, planted in their own season, and they bloom and bear fruit that does not fall to the ground prematurely.

Thought allied fearlessly to purpose becomes creative force. The man who understands this is ready to become something higher and stronger than a mere bundle of wavering thoughts and fluctuating sensations. He who does this becomes the conscious and intelligent wielder of his mental powers.

Insights and Points to Remember

This chapter on *Thought and Purpose* explores the broader implications of positive thinking on our life goals. We learn that lack of purpose can cause feelings of anxiety, self-doubt, fear, and self-pity. A person with no goals or purpose has nothing to fill his time but preoccupation with that very belief—he has no goal or purpose. Convinced of that, he dwells more and more on the futility of his life and sinks deeper into depression and despair.

Life without purpose is like a rudderless sailboat adrift on the sea. It bounces from wave to wave, twisting in the wind, and making random turns that lead to nowhere. Before long, an unlucky sailor may find his boat capsized and his life over.

You may lack purpose at a given moment, but it is only a temporary condition. At these times, you should focus your efforts on the tasks of mundane living to keep your mind engaged and ready to embark upon a great life adventure when it reveals itself.

James Allen writes: "Those who are not prepared to undertake a great purpose should fix their thoughts on the faultless performance of their day-to-day activities…Such focusing is necessary to develop resolution, motivation, and energy. Once this is done, every goal that a man can imagine is within the realm of possibility and can be accomplished."

You may have read wonderful accounts of people who had their life passion revealed in childhood, and it was an easy choice for them to pursue it—indeed, they believe they were born to do so. Others awaken one day with a stunning revelation of what they must do with the rest of their lives; or the knowledge may come to them in other unexpected ways.

You may hear such exciting life stories and think, "I have never felt a dramatic calling. My life has no purpose." But stories of people born to a calling are rare, and most of us are not struck by an electrifying sense of purpose. You may have just a general notion of what you are meant to do in life, or a vague inkling. You might change direction too—a life purpose you love at a young age may lose its luster as you grow up.

Your true purpose and destiny might not be revealed until later in life. Anna Mary Robertson Moses, better known as Grandma Moses, answered a calling to take up painting at the age of seventy-eight. She went on to become a world-renowned American folk artist. Her artwork has been exhibited in many museums, and her drawings have appeared on countless greeting cards. One of her paintings, *The Sugaring Off,* sold for US$1.2 million in 2006.

Inspiration is the force that reveals your life purpose and moves you forward to fulfill your destiny. Any idea that inspires you may become a major goal in your life, or even your crowning achievement if you pursue it. To find a purpose, regardless of your age or position in life, you must listen for, and be able to hear, your inner voice. Your mind must be free of fear and doubt, clear of anxiety and depression, so you can hear the sweet, soft whisper of your soul.

Chapter 6

The Thought-Factor in Achievement

All that a man achieves or fails to achieve is the result of his own thoughts. In an orderly universe governed by natural laws, where loss of equilibrium would mean destruction, individual responsibility is absolute. You cannot blame others for the path you walk when you choose it yourself. All that befalls you along the way, good or bad, is the reward or consequence of your free will. The strengths and weaknesses in your character, your talents and faults, your motivations and fears, are your own and no one else's. They are brought about by your own thinking and not by another. Since you created them, only you can alter them. Your life condition and circumstances are also of your own making and not caused by chance or outside forces. Your suffering and happiness evolve from within.

As you think, so you are.
As you continue to think, so you remain.

A strong and compassionate man will stop on his journey to help a weaker man in need. He will know it is the generous and right thing to do. But he must realize that a strong person cannot help a weaker one unless the weaker is willing to be helped. Even then, the weaker man must learn to become strong himself. He must, through his own efforts, develop the strength he admires in another. No one can alter his condition or instill inner strength but himself.

It is common for us to look around at the world and think, "People are slaves because one man is an oppressor. Let us despise the oppressor." But increasingly today, we see cynical people counter this argument, saying, "That man is an oppressor because many weaker people are willing to be slaves. Let us blame the slaves."

The truth is, the oppressor and slave are collaborators in ignorance and partners in this injustice. One seems to afflict the other, but in reality, they are afflicting themselves. A perfect Knowledge perceives the action of law in the weakness of the oppressed and the abusive power of the oppressor. A perfect Love sees the suffering both conditions involve and condemns neither. A perfect Compassion embraces both the oppressor and the oppressed, for they are the source of each other's torment.

A man who has conquered weakness and can no longer be enslaved, and a man who has given up all selfish thoughts and no longer seeks to enslave, is neither the oppressor nor the oppressed. He is free.

You can only rise, conquer, and achieve by lifting up your thoughts. You can only remain weak, abject, and miserable by refusing to lift up your thoughts.

Before you can achieve anything, even the simplest goals, you must lift your thoughts above the shadows of doubt and fear. To achieve success, you will need to put aside negative thinking and impulsive habits. At the very least, these disruptive thought-seeds will distract you from your goal; at worst, they will sabotage your effort and bring certain failure.

It is not necessary to give up all impulsive behavior and selfish desire to succeed, but at least a portion of it must be sacrificed. If your senses are clouded by doubts or indulgent habits, you cannot think clearly or plan methodically. You will not be able to discover in yourself and develop the abilities and talents required to attain your goal. Without control of your thoughts, you will not be able to control external affairs or take on serious responsibilities. You won't be able to act independently or stand on your own.

There can be no progress and no success without sacrifice. Your success will be in the measure you sacrifice your baser desires and focus your mind on development of your plans. Your success will also depend upon you diverting the energy you were wasting on impure thoughts and indulgent habits to strengthen your resolve and self-reliance. The higher you lift your thoughts, the wiser you will become. The wiser you are, the greater your success and the more enduring your achievements will be.

The Universe does not favor the greedy, the dishonest, the cruel, the depraved, or those others who dwell in the dark shadows of the world. The Law of Karma, which is another way of referring to cause and effect, may seem to work in random, unpredictable ways; and because of that, some people may arrive at the mistaken belief that ours is a chaotic world where the good are punished and the evil rewarded. But in truth, the Universe helps the generous, the honest, the gentle, and the virtuous. All the great Teachers throughout the ages have declared this in innumerable ways. To know it and prove it, you need only persist in making yourself more and more virtuous by lifting up your thoughts.

Intellectual achievements are the result of thought devoted to the search for knowledge, or for what is beautiful and true in life and nature. These accomplishments sometimes come as the result of vanity and ambition, but they are not the outcome of those characteristics. They are the natural outgrowth of long and arduous effort and of pure, unselfish thoughts.

Spiritual achievements are the consummation of divine aspirations. If your thoughts are lofty and spiritual and your mind is fixed on all that is pure and unselfish, then as surely as the sun reaches its zenith and the moon waxes full, you will become wise and virtuous in character. A man who thus becomes wise and virtuous will rise into a position of influence and blessedness.

Achievement, of whatever kind is the result of effort and the ultimate aim of thought. By faithful exercise of self-control and well-directed thought, a man can ascend to the pinnacle of success. By taking the weaker path and yielding to sensuality, indolence, impurity, corruption, and confusion of thought, he falls into the darkness of despair and failure.

A man may achieve great success in the world and reach a lofty altitude in the spiritual realm, yet he may descend again into weakness and failure by allowing arrogant, selfish, and corrupt thoughts to take possession of him. Victories achieved by right thought can only be maintained by watchful vigilance. Many people give way when success is achieved, reverting to old habits and negative ways of thinking, and they rapidly fall back into gloom and failure.

All achievements and successful outcomes, whether moral, intellectual, or material, are the result of definitely directed thought. They are governed by the same law and are of the same method—the only difference lies in the goal pursued or the object of attainment.

A man who desires to accomplish little in life must sacrifice little. He who seeks to achieve much must sacrifice much. The man who seeks to reach the highest and greatest goals must sacrifice greatly.

Insights and Points to Remember

This chapter on *The Thought-Factor in Achievement* explains more about how thought translates into action, and how our thoughts are stepping stones to success or failure. The fact that good thoughts attract success and abundance is discussed. This belief not only appears in the writings of James Allen but in nearly all religions and philosophies dating back to antiquity.

The Taoist scriptures inform us: "Those who are thus, are good: people honor them; Heaven's Reason gives them grace. Blessings and abundance follow them. Bad luck keeps away; angel spirits guard them. Whatever they undertake will surely succeed, and even to spiritual saintliness they may aspire."

The Dhammapada, a Buddhist text written in the third century B.C., provides insights on positive thought and action—the advice is just as relevant today. This text was likely one of James Allen's sources of inspiration. An excerpt follows (T'ai-Shang Kan-Ying P'ien, Translated from Chinese by Teitaro Suzuki and Dr. Paul Carus, *Treatise of the Exalted One on Response and Retribution,* Chicago IL: Open Court Publishing, 1906):

1. All that we are is the result of what we have thought: it is founded on our thoughts, it is made up of our thoughts. If a man speaks or acts with an evil thought, pain follows him, as the wheel follows the foot of the ox that draws the carriage.

2. All that we are is the result of what we have thought: it is founded on our thoughts, it is made up of our thoughts. If a man speaks or acts with a pure thought, happiness follows him, like a shadow that never leaves him.

3. "He abused me, he beat me, he defeated me, he robbed me…" In those who harbor such thoughts, hatred will never cease.

4. "He abused me, he beat me, he defeated me, he robbed me…" In those who do not harbor such thoughts, hatred will cease.

5. For hatred does not cease by hatred in any situation: hatred ceases by love, this is the age-old rule.

6. The world does not know that we must all come to an end here. But those who know it, their quarrels cease at once.

7. He who lives looking for pleasures only, his senses uncontrolled, immoderate in his food, idle, and weak, Mâra (The Temptress) will certainly overthrow him, as the wind throws down a weak tree.

8. He who lives without looking for pleasures, his senses well-controlled, moderate in his food, faithful and strong, Mâra will certainly not overthrow him, any more than the wind throws down a rocky mountain.

9. He who wishes to wear the yellow robe (of the priest) without having cleansed himself of sin, who disregards temperance and truth, is unworthy of the yellow robe.

10. But he who has cleansed himself of sin, who is well grounded in all virtues, and follows temperance and truth, he is indeed worthy of the yellow robe.

11. They who imagine truth in untruth, and see untruth in truth, never arrive at truth but follow vain desires.

12. They who know truth in truth, and untruth in untruth, arrive at truth and follow true desires.

13. As rain breaks through a house with an unsound roof, passion will break through an unreflecting mind.

14. As rain does not break through a well-roofed house, passion will not break through a well-reflecting mind.

15. The evil-doer mourns in this world, and he mourns in the next; he mourns in both. He mourns and suffers when he sees the evil of his own work.

16. The virtuous man delights in this world, and he delights in the next—he delights in both. He delights and rejoices when he sees the purity of his own work.

17. The evil-doer suffers in this world, and he suffers in the next; he suffers in both. He suffers when he thinks of the evil he has done; he suffers more when traveling on the evil path.

18. The virtuous man is happy in this world, and he is happy in the next; he is happy in both. He is happy when he thinks of the good he has done; he is even happier when traveling on the good path.

19. The thoughtless man, even if he can recite a large portion of the law but does not practice it, has no share in the spiritual quest; he is like a cow herder counting the cows of others.

20. The follower of the law, even if he can recite only a small portion of it but has forsaken passion, hatred, and foolishness, possesses true knowledge and serenity of mind. Caring for nothing in this world or that to come, he indeed has a share in the spiritual quest.

It is ironic that despite humanity's glorious achievements and scientific breakthroughs, we still struggle with the ordeal of living from day to day, and we often lose our way on the sea of life as the waves of pessimism and self-doubt rise and fall around us.

Humans are quick to learn from experience. We pass on our knowledge of science, our history, and our culture from one generation to the next. Yet, we rarely learn from the wisdom of others in our daily affairs. We can be told that holding a finger in a flame will burn, yet we do it anyway, sometimes again and again. Only after we have suffered firsthand do we accept that the flame can burn.

Think back to a time when a trusted friend or loved one urged you to follow a particular course of action based on the wisdom of their own experience. Did you heed the advice? If not, did you regret not doing so? Think about how you can be more receptive to sage advice from others who have been able to chart a calm and pleasant journey in life, and from whom we can learn much.

Chapter 7

Visions and Ideals

Dreamers are the saviors of the world. They are the prophets of tomorrow; the agents of inspiration who bestow the gifts of intellect and creativity on the world; the messengers that guide man along the path to truth and enlightenment. As the visible world is sustained by the invisible, so mankind, through all its trials, sins, and sordid fascinations, is nourished by the beautiful visions of its solitary dreamers.

Humanity cannot forget its dreamers. It cannot allow their visions and ideals to fade and die. It lives in them. It knows them in the realities that it will one day see and know. Composer, sculptor, painter, poet, prophet, sage—these are the architects of the afterworld and the pavers of the road to Heaven. The world is beautiful because they have lived. Without them, toiling humanity would wither and perish.

The man who cherishes a beautiful vision or dream in his heart will one day achieve it. Columbus dreamed of a new world and he discovered it. Copernicus had a vision of the universe, and he revealed it. Buddha beheld the vision of a spiritual world of sublime beauty and perfect peace, and he entered into it.

Cherish your visions. Cherish your ideals. Cherish the music that stirs in your heart, the art that colors your mind's eye, and the words of a story you imagine that waits to be told. Cherish the beauty that forms in your mind, the joy that emanates from your purest thoughts. For out of these, will grow all delightful conditions. If you remain true to them, your world will be built.

To desire is to obtain. To aspire is to achieve. There is a difference, and the man in touch with his spiritual being understands it. Desire motivates us to obtain material things; aspiration inspires us to achieve worthy goals. Shall a man's base desires receive the full measure of gratification while his purest aspirations starve for lack of sustenance? Material wealth is temporary and elusive; it disintegrates and becomes nothing. Every material thing that you see around you will fade away. But the soul is immortal and will survive this temporal world, passing beyond it and coalescing with the universe, which is never-ending and eternal.

Be the man who is superior to all others. Seek your highest goals. Aspire to achieve your dreams and reach farther and higher than the common man who toils at meaningless tasks that will be soon forgotten. "Ask and receive," and your aspirations will be realized.

Dream lofty dreams. As you dream, so you will become. Your Vision is the promise of what you shall one day be. Your Ideal is the prophecy of what you will unveil.

The greatest achievements were at first and for a time a dream. The oak sleeps in the acorn; the bird waits in the egg. In the highest vision of the soul, a waking angel stirs. Dreams are the seedlings of realities yet to be discovered and explored.

Your circumstances in life may be vexing, but they will not remain so for long if you perceive an Ideal and strive to attain it. You cannot travel within your being and stand still without.

Here is a young man raised in poverty and hard pressed by life. He lacks education and believes he has no talents or skills worth developing. He labors long hours in an unhealthy workshop. Yet, he dreams of better things. He dwells upon intelligence and focuses his mind on thoughts of refinement, grace, and beauty. He conceives of, and mentally builds up, an ideal condition of life. The vision of a wider liberty and a larger scope takes possession of him, and restless aspiration urges him to action. He uses all his spare time and means, limited though they are, to develop his latent powers and resources. Soon, his mind has become so altered that the confined workshop can no longer hold him. It has become so out of harmony with his mentality that it falls out of his life as a garment is cast aside, and with the growth of opportunities that fit his expanding powers, he leaves it behind forever.

Years later, we see this youth as a grown man. We find him in possession of knowledge, and he is a master of certain forces of the mind he wields with worldwide influence and power. In his hands, he holds the reins of enormous responsibility. He speaks, and in an instant, countless lives are changed. People hang on his words and remold their characters. Sun-like, he becomes the fixed and luminous center around which countless destinies revolve. He has realized the Vision of his youth. He has become one with his Ideal.

You, too will realize the Vision of your heart, be it base or beautiful, or a mix of both—for you will always gravitate toward that which you secretly love the most. In your hands will be placed the exact results of your own thoughts. You will receive what you earn—no more and no less—but the full measure of the effects you have triggered by initiating their underlying causes. Whatever your present environment may be, you will fall, remain, or rise with your thoughts, your Vision, and your Ideal. You will become as small as your controlling desire, or as great as your dominant aspiration.

To quote the beautiful words of Stanton Kirkham Dave:

"You may be keeping accounts, and presently you will walk out of the door that for so long has seemed to you the barrier of your ideals. You will find yourself before an audience, the pen still behind your ear, the ink stains on your fingers, and then and there shall pour out the torrent of your inspiration. You may be driving sheep and you shall wander to the city, bucolic and open-mouthed; you will wander under the intrepid guidance of the spirit into the studio of the master, and after a time, he will say, 'I have nothing more to teach you.' Now you have become the master, who so recently dreamed of great things while driving sheep. You shall lay down the saw and the plane to take upon yourself the regeneration of the world."

The thoughtless, the ignorant, and the lazy, seeing only the apparent effects of things and not the things themselves, talk of luck, fortune, and chance. Seeing a man grow rich they say, "How lucky he is!" Observing another man become intellectual or successful in creative endeavors, they exclaim, "How gifted he is!" Seeing the saintly character and wide influence of another, they remark, "How chance aids him at every turn!"

They do not see the trials and failures or tireless struggles that these men voluntarily underwent to gain their experience. They have no knowledge of the sacrifices they have made, or of the undaunted efforts they have put forth. They have no awareness of the faith they have exercised to overcome seemingly insurmountable hurdles and attain the Vision of their heart. They do not know the darkness and the heartaches; they only see the light and joy, and call it "luck." They do not see the long and arduous journey, but only see the pleasant goal and call it "good fortune." They do not understand the process, but only see the result and call it "chance."

In all human affairs, there are those who make efforts and those who achieve results. In each case, the strength of the effort put forth is the measure of the result. Chance is not a factor, and there are no coincidences in the Universe. So-called gifts, powers, possessions, and attainment, whether material, intellectual, or spiritual, are the fruits of diligent effort: thoughts completed, objectives accomplished, visions realized.

The Vision you glorify in your mind, the Ideal you enthrone in your heart—build your life by this, and this you will become.

Insights and Points to Remember

This chapter on *Visions and Ideals* speaks to us on many levels. It encourages us to dream of a better life and a more peaceful, enlightened world, and to pursue those dreams. We are made aware that dreamers and visionaries are the artists and inventors who add beauty and substance to the world; the leaders who unite the people of their lands and bring nations together in peace; the architects who construct a brighter future for humanity. We are reminded too that honest effort is rewarded, and what abides in our hearts will build the temple of our spiritual destiny.

In every society, we are taught from childhood that success is the reward of hard work, and material wealth is the measure of that success. But is it? Is your purpose in this life to accumulate things and pass away, leaving it all behind to scatter in the wind? If you consider the miracle of the universe in all its vastness, and the triviality of man's pursuit of material things, you will see beyond the illusion of the temporal world and focus a discerning eye on the spiritual world that lies beyond.

Material wealth is worthless if you have lost your health—a sickly man will pass away but cannot take his riches into the next world. Wealth will not bring you happiness, although obsessive pursuit of it can lead to suffering and a wasted life. It will not awaken your spirit or enlighten you, although putting your spirituality aside to pursue material goals will prevent you from developing your higher self. True, without a goal or a dream, we drift aimlessly on the sea of life; but temporal goals do not bring us closer to our spiritual destiny. Material goals are no more than stepping stones on the way to something greater that will ultimately require giving up the things we have accumulated to gain something of greater value to the soul.

A dream or vision does not reveal the big picture. It is but an intriguing glimpse beyond the mundane and into the divine mysteries of the universe. A dreamer who believes his vision is the totality of the answer becomes trapped by the limitations of that dream and will never see beyond it.

A visionary understands that within every dream is the seed of a larger dream waiting to be realized. Thus, dreams are the building blocks of greater dreams, as a castle is built one stone at a time, and the final result consists of many stones skillfully arranged. The dreamer must continue to dream and seek knowledge until the Universe is revealed and he understands the complete vision. This is the path to tranquility and enlightenment.

Chapter 8

Serenity

Calmness of mind is one of the beautiful jewels of wisdom. It is the result of devoted and patient effort in self-control. It is achieved by proper control of the mind and quieting the thoughts. A man can accomplish this in various ways: through relaxation, meditation, and by various other means. A calm mind is a reflection of ripened experience and a much more than ordinary understanding of natural laws and the operations of thought. Calming the mind is the first step to the serenity, deep inner peace, and tranquility that accompanies enlightenment.

You become calm in the measure that you understand yourself as a thought-evolved being. This knowledge helps you understand others as the result of thought. As you develop understanding, and as you see more clearly the intertwining of all things by the action of cause and effect, you will cease to fuss and fume. You will leave anxiety, grief, and fear behind, knowing that these thought forces are agitating, not calming, and by their very nature create more anxiety, grief, and fear. A man who frees himself from this cycle finds that it is easier to remain poised, steadfast, patient, and serene.

The calm man has learned how to govern himself and knows how to adapt to others who notice and admire his dignity, serenity, and spiritual strength. They believe that they can learn from him and rely upon him. He brings calm to all those around him, and the fact that they are calm reinforces the peace and tranquility in his own thoughts and circumstances.

The more tranquil a man becomes, the greater is his success, his influence, and his power for good. Even the ordinary businessman will discover that his prosperity increases as he develops greater self-control and equanimity. He will find that people always prefer to deal with a man whose demeanor is dependable and peaceful.

The strong, calm man is always loved and revered. He is like a shade-giving tree in a thirsty land, a sheltering rock in a storm. Who does not love a tranquil heart and a balanced life? It matters not whether it rains or shines or what changes come to those possessing these blessings, for they are always sweet and serene.

That exquisite state of character we call "serenity" is the final lesson to be mastered in this material world. It is the flowering of life, the fruit of the soul. It is precious as wisdom, more desirable than fine gold. How insignificant money-seeking seems in comparison with a serene life that dwells in the ocean of Truth, beneath the churning waves, beyond the reach of tempests, in the Eternal Calm!

How many people do we know who sour their lives and ruin all that is sweet and beautiful by explosive tempers? How many do we know who destroy their poise of character and make bad blood! It is not a question but a fact that the great majority of people bring havoc into their lives and mar their happiness by lack of self-control. Few people we meet in life are well balanced and possess that exquisite poise owned by the calm, serene finished character!

Humanity surges with uncontrolled passion. Our lives are tumultuous with ungoverned grief, blown about by anxiety and doubt. Only the wise man whose thoughts are controlled and purified makes the winds and the storms of the soul obey him.

Tempest-tossed souls, wherever you may be, and under whatever conditions you may live, know this: In the ocean of life, the isles of Blessedness are smiling, and the sunny shore of your ideal awaits your coming. Keep your hand firmly upon the helm of your thoughts. In the bark of your soul reclines the commanding Master who sleeps. Wake Him! Self-control is strength. Right Thought is mastery. Calmness is power.

Say to your heart: "Peace, be still!"

Insights and Points to Remember

Our topic in this final chapter is Serenity. We are reminded that material wealth can buy luxury, but it does not buy peace of mind. A man can desire good health, but he cannot attain it by sowing unwholesome seeds in his garden. He can pursue knowledge, but without a quiet, tranquil mind to hear life's subtle words of wisdom, the truly important knowledge of life will elude him. Only by embracing the positive and letting go of the negative can he be in harmony with his conditions and discover the great tranquility that permeates the spiritual realm.

Serenity is a state of mind. It begins with acceptance. Thus, the teaching that we should change what can be changed, but accept what cannot be changed, is a guiding principle. Accept and cherish the good that comes to you, learn from the bad, and in this way, you become the master of your life and captain of your destiny. Accept that life is a learning experience and great lessons will be revealed to you. Accept that the material world is a place where material things come and go but the soul is eternal, and you'll begin to understand the meaning of eternity and all those other revelations in the universe that truly matter.

When a man's thoughts are wholesome and his emotions balanced, anxieties and fears about life fall away. He will cease to struggle, and he will conquer failure, because he knows that a properly cultivated garden will bear forth and flourish. When he ceases blind ambition, he will unlock the true power of his own mind and higher being. This power can move mountains; it is constant, infinite, eternal.

A man whose thoughts are positive and whose mind is serene will cease to complain that life is unfair. Such a man will accept that obstacles and setbacks are the seeds of life's lessons, and without them, he would neither learn nor grow. When he encounters resistance, he will know and accept that its purpose is not to frustrate or vex but to strengthen his resolve.

A serene mind is in harmony with the universe. You can

only achieve that blissful state if you flow with the cosmic tide. In doing so, you will find yourself in the right place, at the right time, doing the bidding of your higher self, and fulfilling your spiritual destiny. When your life is in accord with your destiny, all things will happen as they should. Flowing with the tide instead of rowing against, you will cross the sea of life and unlock your glorious potential. The light of your soul will shine bright, and those around you will be blessed by the warm, healing glow of your countenance.

Swimming against the tide will not empower you to cross the ocean; it will only wear you down. Bitter herbs cannot be transmuted into sweet corn, lead cannot be turned into gold. The natural laws are immutable and unerring. We may choose to learn and master them, or ignore them and struggle against them.

The man who sows fertile seeds and tends his garden diligently will be blessed with an abundant harvest. But the man who understands the cycle of the life at work in his garden—the seeds sprout, grow, blossom, and drop their fruit or petals at precisely the right moment—is a knower of truth, and his life will be blessed with harmony, peace, and divine love.

Every great philosophy and religion stresses the value of serenity, and the tools we have to attain it are numerous: meditation, yoga, visualization, breathing techniques, mantras, affirmations, and prayer, among others.

Meditate or pray for what is right, not for what you

want, and your prayers will be answered. Reject doubt and you will conquer it. Embrace hope and your hopes will materialize in reality.

Life is like water, abundant and free flowing, and your body is the glass that contains it. Will you allow your thoughts to agitate the water and cause it to spill? Will you let your emotions churn up the sediment of your fears and anxieties? Or will you calm your hand that holds the glass so it remains full, and calm your mind so the water remains clear and sweet? Every man must make this choice for himself. Your health, your happiness, your life, and your destiny are in your hands. Choose wisely.

Chapter 9

Daily Meditations

This final chapter does not appear in the 1903 version of *As a Man Thinketh*. It presents a collection of thirty empowering affirmations drawn from James Allen's 1913 book, *Meditations for Every Day in the Year*. They can be used to motivate, to achieve inner balance, promote self-healing, or for inspiration. Choose an affirmation that fits your need on a given day and read it aloud; alternatively, read it silently, or use it in a meditation to balance your emotions or focus on positive goals. These excerpts have been edited and restyled for present-day readers.

#1: *Individual selfishness is the common cause of all strife in the world.*

All the activities of human life are rooted in and draw their vitality from one common source: the heart. The cause of all suffering and happiness resides not in the outer activities of human life but the inner activities of the heart and mind. If you cannot endure to have your errors and shortcomings brought to the surface and made known, and you try to hide them, you are not ready to walk the spiritual path of Truth. If you cannot face your lower nature and selfish urges, you are not properly equipped to fight and overcome temptation. To conquer temptation, you must rise to spiritual heights and overcome selfish desire.

#2: *If you seek Truth, you will make the effort necessary for its achievement.*

Meditation is not the same as idle reverie or daydreaming. There is nothing dreamy or unpractical about it. It is a process of searching and uncompromising thought that allows nothing to remain but the simple truth. So, when meditating, you will no longer strive to build your ego, but, forgetting self, you will remember only that you are seeking the Truth. And so you will remove, one by one, the errors you have built around yourself in the past, as you patiently wait for the revelation of Truth. Let the supreme goal of your meditation be Truth.

#3: *Every form of unhappiness springs from a wrong condition or discord in the mind.*

All discord, dis-ease and suffering spring from ignorance—a condition of darkness and lack of inner development. Those who think and act in negative ways in the school of life are like uneducated pupils in the school of learning. They have yet to learn how to think and act in sane and balanced ways. The pupil in learning is not happy doing his lessons wrong, and the student of life cannot escape unhappiness and suffering while negativity exists in their surroundings. Life is a series of lessons. Some of us are diligent in learning them and become pure, wise, and blissfully happy. Others are negligent and do not apply themselves, and they remain unstable and unhappy.

Happiness is mental harmony.

#4: *Purification of the heart comes by focusing the mind on pure things.*

You are a thought-being, and your life and character are determined by the thoughts in which you dwell. By practice, association, and habit, your thoughts tend to repeat with greater ease and frequency, fixing the character in a given direction by producing that automatic action called "habit." By dwelling on pure thoughts every day, you form the habit of pure, enlightened thinking. By the ceaseless repetition of pure thoughts, you become one with those thoughts, and you manifest your attainment in pure actions.

#5: *Self-control will put an end to all sufferings.*

Blessed is the day that you realize you are your own undoer and your own savior. Within yourself is the cause of all your suffering; also within is the source of all peace, enlightenment, and spirituality. Selfish thoughts, impure desires, and acts not shaped by Truth are undesirable seeds from which all suffering springs. Selfless thoughts, pure aspirations, and the sweet acts of Truth are the seeds from which all blessedness grows.

#6: *Impatience is a symptom of impulse and has never helped anyone.*

Devote at least one hour every day to quiet meditation on uplifting subjects and their application to everyday life. In this way, you will cultivate a calm, quiet strength and an optimistic view. Do not be anxious to hurry matters. Do your duty, live a disciplined life, and conquer impulse. Guide your actions by moral and spiritual principles, as distinguished from your feelings, believing that your goal, in its own time, will be accomplished.

#7: Aspiration is longing for spiritual things that exist beyond the physical realm.

Often, the passionate individual is eager to put others right; but if you are a person of wisdom, you put yourself right. If you are eager to reform the world, begin by reforming yourself. The reformation of self does not end with eliminating sensual elements—that is only its beginning. It ends only when every vain thought and selfish aim is overcome. On the wings of aspiration, we rise from ignorance to knowledge, from darkness to light. Without aspiration, we remain bound to the mundane—earthly, sensual, unenlightened, and uninspired. Aspiration is the longing for heavenly things.

#8: Life is what you make it by your own thoughts and deeds.

You attain in the measure that you aspire. Your longing to be is the gauge of what you can be. To fix the mind is to foreordain the achievement. As you can experience and know all low things, so you can experience and know all high things. As you have become human, so you can become divine. Impurity is no more than the impure thoughts of the thinker. Purity is the pure thoughts of the thinker. You cannot think for another. Each individual is pure or impure from their own thoughts and being. To live well and prosper, you must overcome temptation and move your daily affairs out of darkness and into the Light.

#9: *As errors and weaknesses are revealed, purge them.*

Every step you take upward on the spiritual path means leaving something behind and below. The high is reached only at the sacrifice of the low. The good is secured only by abandoning the evil. Knowledge is acquired only by destroying ignorance. Every acquisition has its price. What greatness we forfeit by clinging to old, selfish habits! Behind every humble sacrifice a winged angel waits to bear us up to the heights of knowledge and wisdom. Let the person who has attained spiritual enlightenment guard against falling back. Be careful in small things and be well fortified against temptation and moral error. Aim for the attainment of a perfect life.

#10: *To the spiritually aware, knowledge and love are one and inseparable.*

Love is divine, and when it fills your heart, you will embark on a new life. This Love, this tranquil state of mind and heart, may be sought after and realized by all who are willing, ready, and prepared to enter into a comprehension of all that giving up of the self involves. There is no arbitrary power in the universe, and the strongest chains of fate that bind us are self-forged. We are chained to what causes suffering because we desire to be chained, we love those chains, we think the little dark prison of self is sweet, and we fear that if we leave that prison, we will lose what is real and worth having.

#11: *Those who cling to delusions, self-love, and destructive actions cannot find the Truth.*

Truth brings joy out of sorrow and peace out of turmoil. It points the selfish to the Way of Good, and sinners to the Path of Redemption. Its spirit is the doing of righteousness. To the sincere and the spiritually aware, it brings consolation, and upon those who seek harmony, it bestows peace. Take refuge in Truth, in the Spirit of Good, and in the knowledge and doing of Good. You will be reassured and comforted. Malice will subside, hatred will vanish away. Lust is confined to the nethermost darkness and has no place in Truth's transcendent Light. Be strengthened and comforted, having found refuge in Truth.

#12: *The soul can never find lasting satisfaction except in the attainment of enlightenment.*

Every soul, consciously or unconsciously, hungers for spiritual truth and enlightenment, and every soul seeks to gratify that hunger in its own way, and in accordance with its own state of knowledge. The pathways by which this truth and enlightenment are sought are many. Those who seek consciously are blessed and shall discover the final satisfaction of soul that truth provides. Those who seek unconsciously, although for a time they may bathe in a sea of pleasure, are not blessed; they are creating for themselves pathways of suffering over which they must walk with wounded feet, and the soul will cry out for its lost heritage. Blessed are they who earnestly seek.

#13: *Love is not complete until you live it.*

You cannot know the Real while clinging to the unreal; you cannot live in the light of Truth while clinging to error. As long as you cherish lust, hatred, pride, vanity, and self-indulgence, you can do nothing, for the works that come from these negative elements are perishable. Only when you take refuge in the Spirit of Love within, and you become patient, gentle, pure, and forgiving, will your works bear the fruits of life. The vine is not a vine without its branches, and even then, it is not complete until those branches bear fruit. Practice love daily towards all in heart, mind, and deed. Harbor no impure or destructive thoughts and you will discover the imperishable principle of your being. The only refuge from sin is sinless Love.

#14: *When your soul is clouded with selfishness, you confuse the temporal with the eternal.*

People cling to and gratify the flesh as though it will last forever. They try to forget the nearness and inevitably of its dissolution, but the fear of death and of losing all they cling to clouds their happiest hours. With the accumulation of material comforts and luxuries, your divinity is drugged and you sink deeper into the perishable life of the senses. The perishable in the universe can never become permanent; the permanent can never pass away.

#15: *A listless mind cannot achieve any kind of success.*

Success is rooted in a subtle mental focus on a particular

goal. It subsists in an individual characteristic, or combination of characteristics, and not in a particular circumstance or set of circumstances. Circumstances appear and form part of the success, but these are useless without the mind that can understand and use them. At the root of every success is well-conceived and well-directed energy. The mind has focused upon a project. Success is like a flower—it may appear suddenly, but it is the finished product of a long series of efforts and preparations. Others see the success, but the preparation for it, and the various mental processes that led up to it, are hidden from them. Without exertion, nothing can be accomplished.

#16: *The Universe is eternal because Love is at its heart.*

Positive, enlightened people who abide on higher levels see the Universe and all it contains as the manifestation of one law—the Law of Love. They see love as the molding, sustaining, protecting, and perfecting power ingrained in all living things. To them, love is not only a rule of life, it is the law of life; it is life itself. Knowing this, they order their whole life in accordance with love, regardless of their own personality. By thus practicing obedience to divine love, they become conscious partakers of the power of love, and attain perfect freedom as masters of destiny. Love is perfect harmony, pure bliss, and contains no element of suffering. Refrain from thoughts and actions that are not in accordance with pure love, and all suffering will cease. Love is the only preserving power.

#17: *Energy to be productive must not only be directed towards good ends; it must be controlled and conserved.*

A great Teacher's advice to his pupils, "Keep wide awake!" expresses the necessity for tireless energy if you expect to accomplish your purpose. The advice is equally good to the salesman and the saint. It was the same Teacher who said: "If anything is to be done, do it at once, and attack it vigorously!" The wisdom of this advice is evident when we remember action is creative, and that increase follows upon legitimate use. To get more energy, we must use what we already possess to the fullest. Power and freedom only come to those who put their hands vigorously to some task. Noise and hurry are energy going to waste.

#18: *It is a great delusion that noise means power.*

Where calmness is, there is the greatest power. Calmness is a reflection of a strong, well-trained, disciplined mind. The calm man knows his business; his words are few, but they tell. His actions are well-planned and work true, like an efficient machine. He sees a long way ahead and makes straight for his object. He has anticipated all emergencies and prepared for them. He is never taken by surprise; is never in a hurry; is safe in his dependability, and is sure of his ground. We do not hear working steam—it is the escaping steam that makes a great noise.

#19: *To dwell in good thoughts is to place around oneself an aura of sweetness and power that leaves an impression upon all who come in contact with it.*

As the rising sun chases away the night's shadows, so are all the forces of darkness and negativity put to flight by the pure rays of positive thought that shine from a heart made strong in purity and faith. Where there is sterling faith and uncompromising purity, there is health, success, and power. In such a person, disease, failure, and disaster cannot gain a foothold, for there is nothing to which they can attach. Even physical conditions are largely determined by mental states. The old, materialistic belief that we are what our bodies make us is being replaced by the inspiring belief that we are superior to the body, and the body is what we make it by the power of thought. Every evil in the world has its root and origin in the mind.

#20: *Passion is not power. It is the abuse of power, the dispersion of power.*
When a young man experiencing continual setbacks and misfortunes was mocked by his friends and told to give up further effort, he replied, "Soon you will marvel at my good fortune and success." He knew that he possessed a silent and irresistible power that has taken him through many difficulties and crowned his life with success. If you do not have this power, you may acquire it by practice, and the beginning of this power is likewise the beginning of wisdom. You must start by overcoming pointless trivialities to which you have been a willing victim in the past. Idle gossip and other negative thoughts must be put aside as a waste of valuable energy. Focus on a single aim—have a legitimate and useful purpose, and devote yourself

wholeheartedly to it.

#21: *Where self is, Truth is not; where Truth is, self is not.*

On the battlefield of the human soul, two masters compete for the crown of supremacy and for dominion of the heart: the master of self, called the "Prince of this world," and the master of Truth, called God the Father. The master self is that rebellious one whose weapons are passion, pride, avarice, vanity, ego, and greed. The master Truth is that meek and lowly one whose weapons are gentleness, patience, purity, sacrifice, humility, love. In every soul, the battle is waged, and as a soldier cannot engage at once in two opposing armies, so every heart is enlisted either in the ranks of self or of Truth. There is no half-and-half course. You cannot perceive the beauty of Truth while you look out through the eyes of self.

#22: *What your thoughts are, that is your real self.*

The world and all within it is perceived as your thoughts clothe it. Buddha taught: "All that we are is the result of what we have thought; it is founded on our thoughts; it is made up of our thoughts." So it follows that if you are happy, it is because you dwell in happy thoughts; if miserable, because you dwell in despondent and disabling thoughts. Whether you are fearful or fearless, foolish or wise, troubled or serene, within your soul lies the cause of those states—the cause never comes from without. So you ask, "Do you really mean to say that outward circumstances do not affect our minds?" The infallible truth is:

Circumstances can only affect you as much as you allow. You are swayed by circumstances because you do not have an understanding of the nature, use, and power of thought.

#23: *The overcoming of self is the annihilation of all the elements that produce sorrow.*

The doctrine of overcoming or annihilation of self is simplicity itself. It is so simple and practical that a young child whose mind has not yet become clouded with speculative theories and dogma will be far more likely to comprehend it than many older people who have lost their hold on simple and beautiful truths by embracing complicated beliefs. The annihilation of self requires weeding out and destroying all those elements in the soul that lead to division, strife, suffering, disease, and sorrow. It does not mean the destruction of any good and beautiful or peace-producing quality. The overcoming of self is the cultivation of all the divine qualities.

#24: *When the soul is most tried, its need is greatest.*

Do not despair because of failure. From your failure, you can gain a special greatness and wisdom. No teacher can lead you to that greatness and wisdom more surely and swiftly than your own experience of failure. In every mistake you make, and every time you fall, there lies a lesson of great importance if you look for it. Discover the good in what seems to be disastrous and you will rise superior to every event. Foolish people blame others for their mistakes, but the truth-lover blames only himself. Where temptation is powerful, the greater will be the victory.

#25: *In today's 24 hours, you can become a new person.*

Every day is a new birth in time, holding out new beginnings, new possibilities, new achievements. The ages have witnessed the stars in their orbits, but the present moment of now is timeless. It is a new appearance, a new reality. Each new day heralds a new life and holds out new hopes and opportunities. In these twenty-four hours, you can become a new person. From the old past with its mistakes, failures, and sorrows, you can rise a new being, endowed with power and purpose, and radiant with the inspiration of a new ideal.

#26: *The principles of Truth are fixed and eternal, and cannot be made or unmade by anyone.*

The principles of Truth are discovered by searching and practice. These principles are clear and make the path clearer for other seekers to follow. It is the path along which every human being has traveled who has passed from imperfection to perfection, from discord to harmony. It is the ancient Way along which every saint, guru, and spiritual being has walked to divine perfection, and along which every imperfect being in the future will pass to reach this glorious goal. A person's religion matters not if he is striving daily to discover and follow Truth and purify his heart. While opinions and religions differ, sin does not differ, the overcoming of sin does not differ, and Truth does not differ. Religions change from age to age, but the principles of divine virtue are always the same.

#27: Love is all-inclusive. It refuses to be chained.

By its very nature, Love can never be the exclusive possession of any religion, philosophy, or belief system. To claim to be in exclusive possession of Truth is a denial of Love. Truth is a spirit and a life, and although it may manifest in a wide variety of doctrines, it can never be confined to any one doctrine. Love is a winged angel that refuses to be chained to a particular religion or set of beliefs. Love is above and beyond, outside and greater than all the opinions, doctrines, and philosophies of men. Yet, Love includes all: the righteous and the unrighteous, the fair and corrupt, the clean and unclean. He whose love is so deep and wide as to envelop all people of all creeds and beliefs possesses true wisdom and insight—he knows and sees men as they are. Hatred is the absence of Love and therefore absence of all that is included in Love.

#28: Hasty resolutions are futile. True resolution is the crisis of long thought.

Half-hearted and hasty resolutions are not true resolutions, and they are shattered at the first difficulty. Be slow to form a resolution. Examine your position carefully. Consider every circumstance and possible obstacle you might encounter and be prepared to meet them. Be sure you fully understand the nature of your resolution, your mind is made up, and you have no lingering doubt. With your mind thus prepared, the resolution you reach will be sound, and if you pursue it, you will accomplish your strong purpose.

#29: Evil is an experience and a condition, not a power.

If evil were an independent power in the universe, it could not be transcended by any being. Though not real as a power, it is real as a condition, an experience. It is a state of ignorance and lack of spiritual development. Evil retreats and disappears before the light of knowledge. The painful experiences of evil pass away as the new experiences of good enter your field of consciousness.

#30: People of real power and influence are few.

It is easy for a person, surrounded by the comfort of their possessions, to become convinced that they embrace and follow the principles of Peace and Universal Love. But when these possessions are threatened, or the person imagines they are threatened, they clamor for war and show that they believe not in Peace and Love but strife and selfishness. The man who does not desert his principles when threatened with the loss of every earthly thing, even his own life, is the man of power, whose every word endures, and whom the afterworld honors, reveres, and worships. Spiritual power cannot be acquired except by that inward illumination and enlightenment.

-end-

About the Editor

Richard De A'Morelli published his first article in a national magazine at age 14 and signed a multi-book contract with a brick-and-mortar publisher at 18. Since then, he has written and published fifteen nonfiction books, including two best sellers in the self-help field and two English grammar best sellers.

Beyond writing, Richard has three decades of experience as a professional editor. He was a bylined editorial staff member to the late Irving Wallace, one of the top-selling authors of the late twentieth century, and he has worked as Senior Editor and Managing Editor with print and digital media publishers. His author clients have affectionately nicknamed him "Jedi Editor" for his work on books that include *Apocalypse Orphan* by Tim Allen, a 2016 science-fiction bestseller on Amazon, and *Eden's Serum* by Angelique Anderson.

Richard worked a five-year stint as a journalist in southern California, publishing over 500 newspaper, magazine, and tabloid features under his byline. He taught journalism and creative writing at Los Angeles Valley College and Learning Tree University in Northridge, California, and he developed twelve online writing courses for Virtual University. His recent books include:

Elements of Style 2017
Elements of Style: Classic Edition
Quick & Easy English Punctuation
Live Well. Be Happy.

Readers wishing to follow or contact the author about his books or professional editing services can do so on these websites:

Author's Website:	https://spectrum.org/richard
Facebook Profile:	https://facebook.com/writer2
Facebook Page:	https://facebook.com/jedi.editor
Twitter:	https://twitter.com/Jedi_Editor
Instagram:	https://instagram.com/jedi_editor/

A Message from the Publisher

If you liked this book...

Good reviews help spread the word to other readers. If you enjoyed this book, please take a minute to visit your favorite online bookstore and post a review. Even a few words saying you liked the book will be appreciated!

Subscribe to Our Free Mailing List

Subscribe to our free newsletter and be among the first to know about new books from Spectrum Ink, author interviews, discount coupons, and more. Subscribe today at https://spectrum.org/books/popsubscribe.html

More Books from Spectrum Ink

Elements of Style 2017
(Nonfiction Reference/Writing)

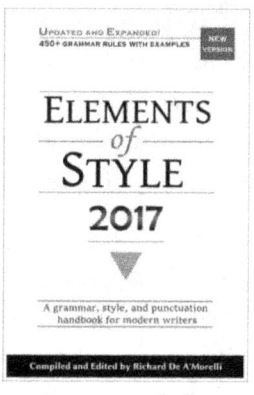

Elements of Style 2017 provides a convenient, all-in-one reference to modern grammar, style, and punctuation rules. Clear, concise writing is essential in today's world. For a writer, a well-edited manuscript may bring an acceptance letter from a publisher or agent; or for a self-published author, it could generate positive reviews and boost sales. For students, an impressed instructor could mean an A grade; and on the job, a well-written report could mean a pay raise, a promotion, or the success of a business venture.

Learn how to improve your grammar and style, and polish your writing to perfection with *Elements of Style 2017*.

Buy online or visit: http://spectrum.org/books/elements

ISBN Number	Edition
978-1-988236-26-1	MOBI/Kindle
978-1-988236-27-8	EPUB Digital
978-1-988236-28-5	Paperback
978-1-088236-31-5	Paperback (Retail)

Live Well. Be Happy.
by Richard De A'Morelli
(Inspirational/Self-Help)

This book is about your life and your search for happiness. It will help you to realize that you can change your life by changing how you think and react to the world around you. You will learn steps you can take to stay positive and balanced in a crazy world and discover how making simple changes in your daily routine can help you find your path to happiness.  You'll also explore simple methods to reduce stress, overcome depression, conquer unhealthy habits, and stay balanced using natural techniques such as deep relaxation, visualization, rhythm breathing, and meditation.

If you have been looking for a book that will encourage you to change your life and give you a helping hand to move forward, this short course in modern living may be that inspiration. The book also makes a wonderful gift for someone in need of encouragement and a step-by-step approach to getting their life on a positive track.

Buy online at: http://spectrum.org/books/live-well/

978-1-988234-09-3	MOBI/Kindle
978-0-993634-08-6	EPUB Digital
978-1-988234-04-8	Paperback
978-1-988236-46-9	Paperback (Retail)

Notes

Notes

Notes

Notes

Notes

Notes

Notes

www.ingramcontent.com/pod-product-compliance
Lightning Source LLC
Chambersburg PA
CBHW070121080526
44586CB00013B/1351